Chapter 1: A Three Month Walk—A Three Month Wait

IT WAS THE THIRD NEW MOON
AFTER THE ESCAPE FROM EGYPT—
ON THE DAY
THAT THE FAMILIES OF ISRAEL JOURNEYED FROM THEIR CAMP AT REFIDIM
TO THE WILDERNESS OF SINAI AND CAMPED THERE.

From the Torah: Exodus 19:1

In the first few weeks after leaving Egypt, your life changed completely. For the first time in your life you were free. What were your first adventures? What was it like to have escaped slavery? To be on the way to becoming a people and finding a nation?

FRIENDS' IN FREEDOM

Erika: I worked sewing clothes for the Egyptians.

Danny: I worked building scaffolds which other Jews used to build with the bricks they had made. Erika and I didn't know each other then. We maybe had seen each other only once or twice, but we didn't know each other at all. We met on the way out, near the Reed Sea. Her little sister tripped when everyone was running, and I picked her sister up and carried her on my shoulders. Later that day, Erika and I talked non-stop for almost the whole night.

Erika: The whole day we were scared. We were sure that we were going to be caught. We knew for a fact that some of us would die. But, we were wrong—that didn't happen. Everyone made it. The Exodus was the perfect rescue mission.

Danny: She was scared; I had faith. When I was a slave, I didn't have any friends. Erika might have worked with other girls and talked to them when she was sewing, but I was working alone all day on the scaffolds.

Jason: When we were slaves, the taskmasters kept us from really talking to each other. In Egypt, we were acquaintances, not friends. No one trusted or helped anyone else—there was too much risk. That was a mistake. Danny, Erika and I became friends on the journey—when we knew that we needed each other. Our fears had kept us from being friends earlier.

CHANGING FEELINGS

Kent: When I was a slave in Egypt I was a brickmaker. Sometimes I did what I was told, but when I didn't I was beaten. That happened a lot.

The first night out of Egypt, I went looking for a friend. I didn't know where my family was—and I didn't want to be alone. I needed someone to talk to. That night I really believed that we were going to get away, that in the future everything would be great. Everybody else was happy and hopeful, too.

Two weeks later, that feeling—that everything was going to be great—I didn't feel it nearly as much, but I still hoped that things would work out. Things had become really hard. Water was short. There wasn't a lot of food. I wasn't sure then that freedom with hunger was better than well-fed slavery, but still I hoped.

After God fed us with manna, I knew that we were going to go on, that it would be all right. Other people thought that this might only be a one time thing. But I knew that God was going to continue to take care of us.

For the first week and a half or so, everyone got along, but people got mean as they got hungry. Soon, there was a lot of fighting. People didn't share. Everyone was used to taking orders and none of us really knew how to take care of ourselves. We had to learn how to work together. Every time someone would try to organize and lead, everyone else would complain, "You're not the boss over us." It took a long time to become a group.

SAVING THE LAST JEW

Danny: I started out falling behind. I shouted out to an empty wilderness, "Come on, guys, wait up—I can't go any farther. God, give me a camel, please." A few days later I said to myself, "I can still see them, sort of, way off in the distance. No, I don't see them anymore." I slept during the day and tried to follow their tracks at night. I was lost in the desert—left behind—never to be found again.

Joel: After the attack by Amalek, after we were defeated, I took a bunch of my students back to look for stragglers and survivors. I found Danny lying way back in the sand—he was barely alive. When I realized that we had lost him earlier, that we had let him slip away, I felt really bad. It taught me that we have to be careful and worry about keeping each and every Jew with us. If we had lost Danny, we'd have lost something irreplaceable.

In the three months since leaving Sinai...

Shane L.: I now have more belief in God. But along the way, my faith was on and off. I was never really sure. Now I fully trust—but when we were in slavery, I didn't really believe in anything.

Shane P.: I learned how to work with other people—how to be united—also how to fight together, how to defend ourselves, and how to work without taking orders.

David S.: I'm stronger now. My legs are stronger from all that walking. I am also a stronger person. I have a lot more will power. I didn't feel too good about myself when I was a slave. Now that's different.

David V.: I've learned that if you believe, that if you put your mind to something, you can usually accomplish it.

Davida: When I was a slave, I sort of wanted to die, because I hated it. But now, I am happy that I am alive.

Ben: I am a better person. I wasn't honest when I was a slave. I lied, and stole, and cheated—all to take care of myself, my friends, and my family. Now I spend a lot of time helping work things out. Now that we've escaped, people don't tell you what to do. Instead, they just tell you what they need.

Kent: I feel like I can open up a little. In Egypt, I was afraid to say anything—afraid to even talk to anybody. Right before we escaped from Egypt, I just got fed up with it. I started to defy. I felt like I was dying and everything was falling apart. When we were leaving, I just turned around and started saying, "Hello. What's your name? My name is Kent." to everybody. I wanted to get to know everyone, all 600,000. Now I know, maybe, ten of them.

Erika: Before, when I was a slave, I was always afraid of being killed. Now, I feel more confident about myself.

It took almost three months to go from Egypt to Mt. Sinai. In those three months how did you change? How were you more ready to receive the Torah? How were you more ready to enter into the covenant?

____

____

____

____

____

____

Why did God wait three months to give the Torah to Israel?

THE COVENANT WAS NOT MADE UNDER DURESS

There is a Jewish law which teaches that if a master wants to free a non-Jewish slave so that she can become his wife, the master must first free her, then let her live as a free Jewess for three months. After she has had time to decide (and is no longer marrying her master just to become free), the wedding may take place.

After God freed the families of Israel from Egyptian slavery, God waited three months before making the covenant at Mt. Sinai. The giving of the Torah was like a wedding between God and Israel. Israel promised to worship only One God, and God promised to make Israel into God's Treasured People.

Just like a king who was marrying a princess, God sent many gifts to Israel before the wedding: "manna which fell like dew, water which gushed from rocks, and even flocks of quail for meat."

From the Midrash: Pesikta D'Rav Kahana 12, 106a

IT TAKES TIME TO LEARN HOW TO USE FREEDOM

God had originally planned to give the Torah to Israel as soon as they were free. But, when Israel first left Egypt, there was a lot of fighting and arguing with each other. People were not getting along. After three months of marching together in the wilderness, and learning that they needed to depend on each other, people began to get along.

Then God said in words which would become Proverbs 3:17-8: "THE TORAH'S WAYS ARE BEAUTIFUL, ALL ITS PATHS ARE PEACE." Then God knew Israel was ready for the Torah.

From the Midrash: Pesikta D'Rav Kahana 12, 106a

Chapter 2: God Chooses the Families of Israel

WHILE THE FAMILIES OF ISRAEL CAMPED AT THE FOOT OF THE MOUNTAIN
MOSES WENT UP TO GOD.
ADONAI CALLED TO HIM FROM THE MOUNTAIN, SAYING:
"SAY THIS TO THE HOUSE OF JACOB
AND TELL THIS TO THE FAMILIES OF ISRAEL—
'YOU HAVE SEEN FOR YOURSELVES
THAT WHICH I DID TO THE EGYPTIANS
AND HOW I CARRIED YOU ON THE WINGS OF EAGLES
AND BROUGHT YOU TO ME.
SO, NOW—
IF YOU WILL LISTEN, LISTEN CAREFULLY TO MY VOICE
AND IF YOU WILL KEEP MY COVENANT
YOU WILL BE THE PEOPLE WHO ARE A TREASURE
(OUT OF ALL THE PEOPLES)...
YOU WILL BE A NATION OF KOHANIM
AND A HOLY PEOPLE.'
SPEAK THESE WORDS TO THE FAMILIES OF ISRAEL."

From the Torah: Exodus 19:2-6

The holiday of Shavuot celebrates the day when Israel received the Torah. One of its Hebrew names is H̲ag Matan Torah, the holiday of the giving of the Torah.

One H̲asidic teacher asked, "Why was it called the holiday of the giving of the Torah and not the holiday of the receiving the of Torah?"

He answered his own question: "God gave the Torah equally to all Jews, but each of us received it differently, according to our skills, our ability, and our attitude."

How were you ready to receive the Torah? What is there about your character or attitude which makes you a good person to bring the Torah to life and to pass it on to others?

____

____

____

Kent: Can I go first? I think I am a good person for this, because a lot of times the Torah speaks about enemies. Back then, we needed leaders to help protect us. In a small way, during the walk from Egypt, I was a semi-leader. I think that I helped to keep other people moving and make people feel like they weren't the only idiot walking in this desert.

David V.: Because I decided to become a bar mitzvah. I've decided to continue my studies.

Shane P.: I think that I am a good candidate, not that I'm good for it, but because I need it. I can learn a lot from it. I can become wiser and more knowledgeable.

Shane L: Because now I am ready to take on some responsibility.

Why did God pick Israel to be the only nation who would receive the Torah?

ONLY ISRAEL WOULD ACCEPT THE TORAH

God offered the Torah to each of the nations of the world, so that none of them could say, "Had we been asked, we might have accepted it."

Adonai came to the first nation and said to them: "Will you accept the Torah?" They asked, "What is written in it?" God said, "Do not murder." They said, "No thank you."

Then Adonai came to the next nation and said to them, "Will you accept the Torah?" They asked, "What is written in it?" God said, "Do not commit adultery." They said, "No thank you."

Then Adonai came to a third nation and said to them, "Will you accept the Torah?" They asked, "What is written in it?" God said, "Do not steal." They said, "No, thank you."

Finally, Adonai came to the families of Israel and said to them; "Will you accept the Torah." With out asking a question they said, "Na'aseh V'nishmah." We will do and we will listen."

Most nations of the world wouldn't even accept the seven mitzvot God gave to Noah for all peoples to follow. But Israel accepted all 613 mitzvot in the Torah, even before they heard them. They said "Na'aseh" (we will do the Torah) before they said, "V'nishmah" (we will listen to the Torah).

From the Midrash: Mekhilta, ba-Hodesh, Yitro 5

EVEN ISRAEL NEEDED TO BE PERSUADED

The Torah says: (Exodus 19:17) AND MOSES BROUGHT THE PEOPLE OUT OF THE CAMP TO MEET WITH GOD, AND THE PEOPLE WAITED UNDER THE MOUNTAIN. It is possible that you might think that "UNDER THE MOUNTAIN" meant "AT THE FOOT OF THE MOUNTAIN." You are wrong—it really does means "UNDER THE MOUNTAIN." From these words we learn this midrash:

The Holy-One-Who-Is-To-Be-Praised lifted up Mt. Sinai and held it over the heads of the families of Israel like an open casket. God said, "If you accept the Torah, good! If not, this is your burial place."

The families of Israel then said: "Na'aseh V'nishmah."

A Midrash from the Talmud: Shabbat 88a

GOD DEMANDS A GUARANTEE

When you take out a loan, a guarantor is the person who will "co-sign" the contract and guarantee that you will keep your side of the deal. Before God made a covenant with Israel and agreed to give them the Torah, God demanded guarantors.

Even though the families of Israel wanted the Torah, God still wasn't sure. God said to them, "I can't give you the Torah unless you bring me guarantors who will assure that you will follow its laws."

Israel said, "Master of the Universe, our ancestors, the patriarchs and matriarchs, will be our guarantors."

But God said, "I can find fault with each of them. For example: Abram doubted My word and said (in Genesis 15:8), "HOW DO I KNOW THAT I WILL REALLY INHERIT IT?" Isaac would have given away the leadership of the Jewish people to Esau, a son who had idols in his house. And Jacob said (in Isaiah 15:27) "Adonai doesn't know everything. I do." God then said, "I need better guarantors."

Israel then spoke up, "Master of the Universe, our prophets will be guarantors." God said, "I find fault with them, too. In the future, you will not always listen to their word. If you won't accept their word, why should I?" God said once again: "I need better guarantors."

This time, the families of Israel said, "Master of the Universe, our children will be the guarantors." God said, "They will do." At that moment, all the pregnant women stepped forward. God spoke to the unborn children in their wombs and said, "I will give the Torah to your parents if you will serve as their guarantors." They said, "Na'aseh V'nishmah."

From the Midrash: Song of Songs R. 1.4

Chapter 3: At the Foot of Mt. Sinai

MOSES RETURNED.
HE GATHERED
THE ELDERS OF THE PEOPLE.
HE PLACED BEFORE THEM
ALL THE WORDS
WHICH *ADONAI*
HAD COMMANDED.

ALL THE PEOPLE ANSWERED
TOGETHER AS **ONE**
AND SAID,
"ALL THAT *ADONAI* HAS SPOKEN,
WE WILL DO."

MOSES THEN BROUGHT
THE PEOPLE'S WORDS
BACK TO *ADONAI*.

From the Torah: Exodus 19:7-8

Why did God choose Mt. Sinai as the place to give the Torah?

All the mountains heard that God was going to give the Torah to Israel. Every mountain was trying hard to be chosen—every mountain but one.

Mt. Everett came to God and said, "I am the tallest mountain in the world. The Torah is important. It should be given from the highest, most important place on earth." God thought, "Boy, is this mountain conceited!" But, God said, "Thank you, but I'm not sure I can have Moses using an oxygen mask and Sherpa guides to get the Ten Commandments. Don't call us, we'll call you."

Next came Miss Poconos, the most beautiful mountain in the whole range of Poconos Mountains. She said, "See here, God, the Torah is the most important thing You've got. You should give it on a real babe of a mountain, a mountain like me." God thought, "This mountain is really stuck up. But, God said: "Thank you, Miss Poconos, we're looking for a different type, but we'll keep you in mind (as a last resort). Don't call us, we'll call you."

Every single mountain was raising its hand. Every single mountain was jumping up and down. Every single mountain wanted to be chosen. Every single mountain—except one.

The next mountain was the Matterhorn, a very important, very sophisticated mountain. He said, "My dear God, this Torah scroll of yours is a work of art. It needs the proper setting. You need a suave, continental mountain, a mountain with class, a mountain just like me." God thought, "another ego-tripping mountain." But God said, "I'm sorry, my dear Matterhorn, but you've already agreed to be a ride at Disneyland. I can't have Moses waiting in line to buy an "E" ticket. Don't call us..."

God was getting desperate. The right mountain had to be out there somewhere.

"My name is Mt. Rushmore. Here is my re´sume´. I am made out of granite, and they carve important faces in me. We could have your picture carved right over there…." God said, "My image! That's against the commandments. Don't call us."

Mountain after mountain came forward. Mt. Ararat, the resting place for Noah's ark. Mt. Gilboa, the place where Debora defeated the Canaanites. It seemed that every single mountain had come before God, and none of them was right. All of them were shouting: "Me! Me! Choose Me. I'm the best. Me!" God didn't know what to do. Then God saw Mt. Sinai standing quietly off to the side, not saying anything.

God asked, " What is your name?" The mountain answered, "Why, Sinai, your Godliness." "Don't you want to be the Chosen Mountain, Mt. Sinai?"

Mt. Sinai answered, "But…but…but…I'm just a little unimportant mountain. Someone else should be chosen."

At that moment, God knew that Mt. Sinai was the perfect mountain. God thought, "Mt. Sinai is wonderful—Mt. Sinai cares about everyone else." It was at that moment that God sent for the Torah.

From the Midrash: (An Original Reworking of) Midrash Aseret ha-Dibrot

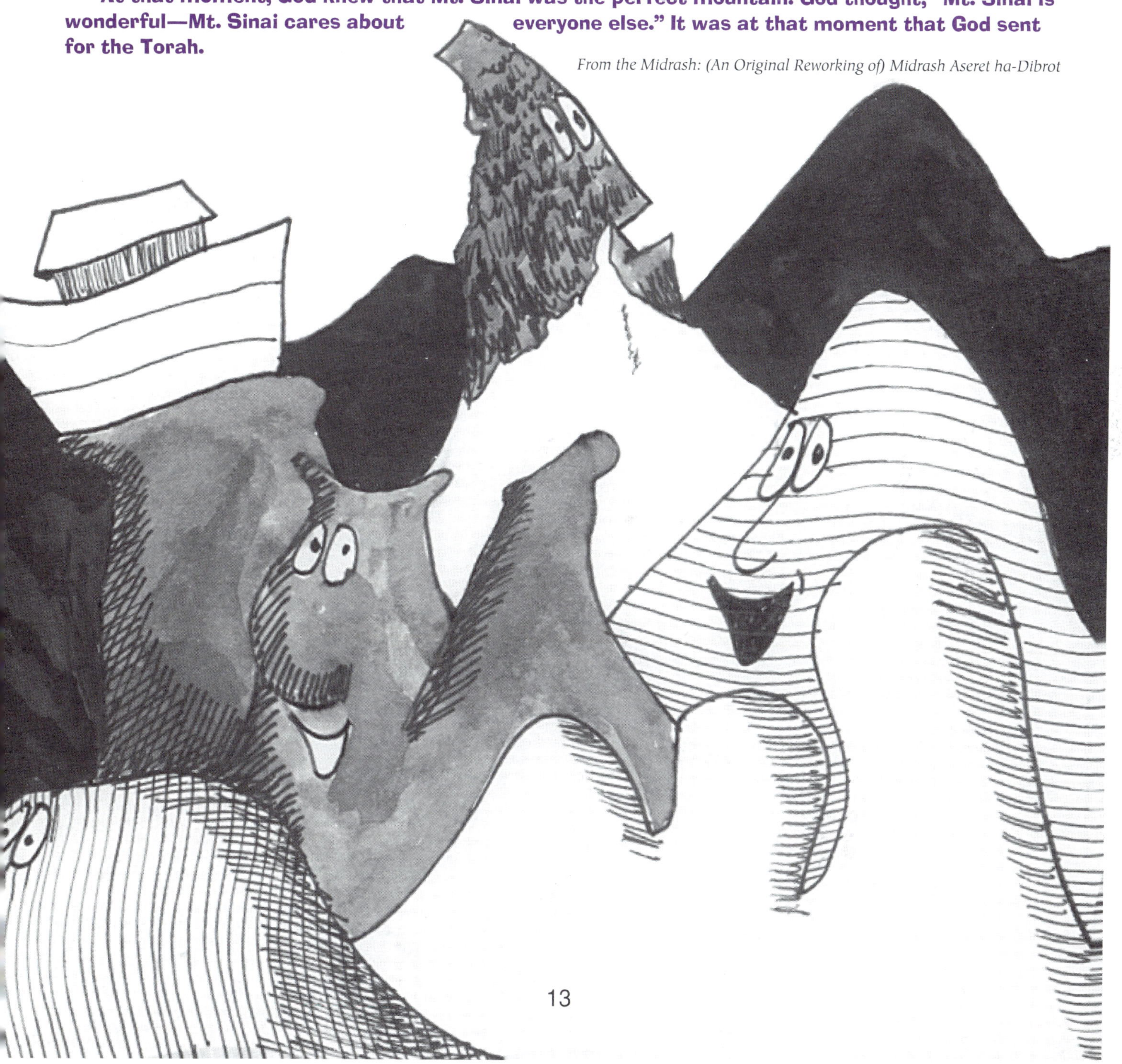

In the original midrash only Mt. Gilboa, Mt. Tavor, and Mt. Ararat were mentioned. Joel added the others when he rewrote the midrash. What mountain would you add to this story? How would that mountain argue? What would God respond?

Name of mountain: ____

____

Why does that mountain want to be picked? _________________________

____

____

Why does God turn it down? ______________________________________

____

____

Chapter 4: Waiting

ADONAI SAID TO MOSES:
"HERE—I AM COMING TO YOU FROM A THICK CLOUD
SO THAT THE PEOPLE CAN HEAR WHEN I SPEAK WITH YOU
AND SO THAT THEY WILL BELIEVE YOU FOREVER."
MOSES THEN TOLD THE PEOPLE'S WORDS TO ADONAI.

ADONAI SAID TO MOSES:
"GO TO THE PEOPLE—
MAKE THEM HOLY TODAY AND TOMORROW HAVE THEM WASH THEIR CLOTHES
AND THEY WILL BE READY ON THE THIRD DAY—
BECAUSE ON THE THIRD DAY ADONAI WILL COME DOWN
BEFORE THE EYES OF THE WHOLE NATION ON MT. SINAI.

Exodus 19:9-11

The Midrash teaches (Exodus Rabbah 28.5) that every Jew who ever lived and who ever will live was at Mt. Sinai. When you were standing, waiting for the Torah, whom did you see? To whom did you talk?" Name five Jews whom you saw at Sinai:

____

____

Pick one of those Jews and think of three questions you would like to ask him or her.

1. ____

2. ____

3. ____

Imagine how the Jew you chose to meet at Sinai would answer those three questions:

____

____

____

____

____

____

____

____

MEETING ANNE FRANK

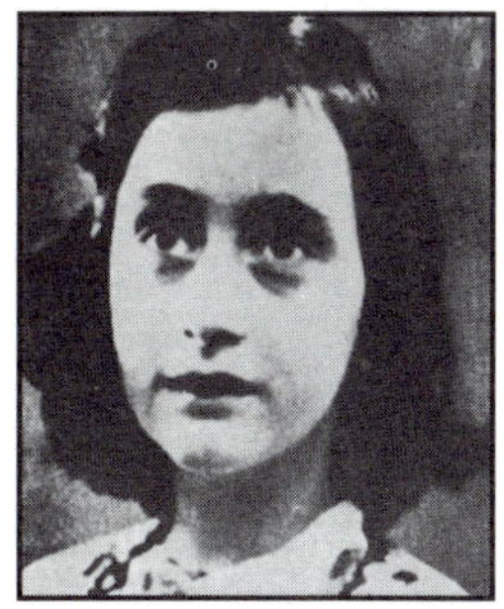

Davida: When I stood at Mt. Sinai, waiting for the Torah, I met Anne Frank. I asked her about the attic. She said, "It was smelly and cramped. We lived there for a long time. We had to be very quiet so that no one would hear us. I wrote in my diary a lot. I wanted to be free so much. I wanted to feel the breeze on my face and roll in the grass. But since I couldn't leave the attic, I drew pictures instead." I asked her, "How was it living in the concentration camp?" She said, "It was very scary because I knew I was going to die there. My whole family except for my father had died. I felt all alone. I felt so much hate for Hitler and his supporters. I couldn't believe that one man could be so evil."

I asked her, "How could you stand it? How did you keep from going mad?" "I sort of had this thing that I repeated to myself: 'I am going to get out. I am going to be okay.' I said that over and over. I tried to imagine myself out of there." I knew that Anne Frank had written: "It's really a wonder that I haven't dropped all my ideals, because they seem so absurd and impossible to carry out. Yet, I keep them because of everything I still believe that people are really good at heart." I asked how she could have written that after all that happened to her. She said, smiling, "Before I went into the attic, I knew a lot of people who were nice and good—and I knew that even though Hitler was evil, there were still lots of other good people left. After all, the family who risked their own lives to hide us, proved that people were good."

Finally, I asked her, "Do you believe in God?" She said, "Yes." My last question was, "Then how do you think God let this happen?" She answered, "I don't know. I guess it is something God doesn't control. I know that God is all-powerful and everything—but, God created us and doesn't control what people do." Shane was standing next to us. He said, "God was taking a nap." Anne answer him quietly, "No, God was there with me."

PLAYING CATCH WITH SANDY KOUFAX

Brett: At Mt. Sinai, while we were waiting, I got to toss a ball around with Sandy Koufax, the Jewish strike-out king who pitched for the Dodgers from 1959 to 1966 and who set the record of 15 strike-outs in a single world series game against the New York Yankees in 1963.

I asked him, "How did you get interested in baseball?" He answered, "Well, when I was a little kid I used to play catch with my dad. Catch turned into pitching practice." Then I asked, "Did you expect to make it big in the major leagues?" "Not really," Sandy said, "It just happened." I think he was just being modest. Next, I got to my big question: "When there was a world series that fell on Yom Kippur, how come you chose not to pitch?" He said, "It fell on the most special of Jewish holidays—and it wouldn't have been right to play. I felt like I would have let all Jews down if I did." I was really curious about his decision, so I asked him, "Did you really, really want to play in that game?" "Yes," he said without hesitating, "I did, but it just wasn't the right thing to do. I didn't want to let my religion down." "Were people angry at you?" I asked. "Personally, I don't care," Sandy went on, "because in my heart I knew I did the right thing."

The last question just came to me. I asked Sandy, "Are you a good Jew?" He said, "I don't know." I answered for him, "Well, Sandy, I think you are."

THE PEARLMAN FAMILY COUSINS CLUB MEETS AT MT. SINAI

Shane: While I was waiting for the Ten Commandments to start, I decided that I wanted to meet my ancestors. I took a big sheet of papyrus and wrote on it, "Pearlman Family Meet Here." It was amazing—hundreds and hundreds of Pearlmans gathered around the sign. We all kept trying to figure out who was related to whom and how.

I met this guy Lefty Pearlman who came from the time of Moses. When he was in Egypt, being a Jew didn't mean much to him—it was only negative. He left Egypt with Moses, not so much because he believed in God, or because being a Jew was important, but because there was a slight chance for freedom. That all changed in the wilderness after he experienced what God could do.

Then I met a woman who was a housewife in Troyes, France. After all, my family is French. Her husband was one of Rashi's students. I asked her if she had kids. She said, "Of course. You wouldn't be here if I didn't." Her husband was a wine merchant and spent a lot of time studying at Rashi's academy. One of my uncles who was nearby explained that in those days, studying with Rashi was like going to Harvard University. This relative of mine (whose name I don't remember) told me she was proud of her husband and had a wonderful life.

Next, I met "Billy the Pearlman," a Jewish gunslinger from the Wild West, a relative of Wyatt Earp's wife (who was also Jewish). But, just as we started to talk, God interrupted us with the Ten Commandments.

A SURVIVOR'S STORY

Kent: I wound up listening to a Holocaust survivor tell his story. "It was more than hard," he said. "It was a day to day struggle to stay alive. Even though the food was scarce and it was very hard—the experience also bonded people together. You were always dependent on some one else. If you didn't associate yourself with other people, you felt like there was nothing to live for. But I always felt like I had something to live for. I felt that way, because I wasn't going to let Judaism just die. I felt that it was my responsibility to live and keep others alive." At that point I asked the survivor: "How did it feel to you when you thought that the Jewish religion was going to die?" "I didn't," he answered. "I knew that God didn't choose us to have all this historic stuff happen to us—like at Sinai and in Egypt—just to watch us die because a crazy man hated us. I just wasn't going to die. I couldn't let myself die. I couldn't let people around me die. I felt that we couldn't let it end with us."

ALBERT EINSTEIN

Danny: I met Albert Einstein and Andrew Dice Clay. They were both comedians. After Andrew Dice Clay told a few jokes, Einstein entertained the crowd by taking off his vest without taking off his jacket. He said it was a mathematical principle. I asked Dr. Einstein how he could have let the world know about his theory when he knew it would lead to the atom bomb and all that damage and destruction. He reached into his pocket and took out a pocket knife. He asked me what it was and I said, "A knife." He asked me, "Is this knife good or bad?" I said, "It depends on who uses it and what they do with it." He said, "It is the same with my understandings of time and space—it depends on who uses it and what they do with it. Hitler had to be stopped—but I never imagined the amount of destruction and death that would result." Later, while Andrew Dice Clay was telling more jokes, I heard Einstein arguing with someone about God. Einstein said, "Nothing which was created was an accident. After all, God doesn't play dice with the universe." When the Diceman told his next joke, Einstein looked up and said, "Maybe God does!"

Chapter 5: The Revelation

MOSES BROUGHT THE PEOPLE FROM THE CAMP TO MEET GOD.
THEY STOOD AT THE BOTTOM OF THE MOUNTAIN.

MT. SINAI WAS ALL SMOKE, BECAUSE *ADONAI* CAME DOWN IN FIRE.
THE SMOKE ROSE LIKE THE SMOKE OF A FURNACE.
THE WHOLE MOUNTAIN SHOOK—A LOT.

THE VOICE OF THE SHOFAR WAS GROWING VERY STRONG—
MOSES KEPT SPEAKING— AND GOD KEPT ANSWERING IN A VOICE.

ADONAI CAME DOWN ON THE MOUNTAIN TO THE TOP OF THE MOUNTAIN.

ADONAI SAID ALL THESE THINGS:

From the Torah: Exodus 19:17-20:

What was it like for you when the Torah was actually given? What did you see? What did you hear? What did you feel? What did you believe? What did you promise?

____

____

____

____

What was it like during the revelation at Sinai?

Shane L: When I was standing at Mt. Sinai, I saw a tube of fire going up and down from the mountaintop to heaven. I heard great words spoken through this tube. Smoke was everywhere. I remember that I was astounded by what it looked like. God's Voice was a big booming sound. God had great bass reproduction.

Shane P: I sort of heard echoes everywhere. Like the words being spoken over and over and over and over again to everyone.

David S: I think the voice was very deep. The mountain shook from the vibrations of this deep voice.

Kent: I didn't hear anything. There was a little shake, but I heard nothing. Everybody else was staring up—waiting for something to happen. We saw the flashes in the sky, but I heard nothing.

Danny: I just remember confusion.

Erika: It was weird. It was like it wasn't real. It was like a movie with special effects. I heard kind of like thunder and lightning—a rumbling. The voice sounded like a phonograph record which was pushed around at the wrong speed by hand. It all happened in slow motion.

Jason: When I heard God's voice—which was really, really low—I promised that I wouldn't fight with my brothers anymore.

Brett: What I remember most is a whole bunch of people and all the yelling and all the excitement.

Andy: It was exciting. God's Voice sounded like my father's.

NOTHING UP THIS SLEEVE

Just before giving the Ten Commandments, God sent Moses back down the mountain. God wanted to make sure that all the members of the families of Israel heard the commandments directly. And, God wanted to make sure that all Israel knew that the Torah came from God and not Moses. When God began, "I AM ADONAI YOUR GOD,"no one suspected that Moses might be speaking.

From the Midrash: Exodus Rabbah 28: 3

GOD HAS GREAT BASS

It was night. God came down on Mt. Sinai in a ball of fire. The earth quaked. There was thunder and lightning. The families of Israel heard the sound of the shofar becoming louder and louder, until it almost broke their ear drums. The fire on Mt. Sinai rose up to the heavens, and the mountain smoked like a furnace. The families of Israel trembled with fear.

From the Midrash: Mekhilta, Yitro: 1, 57a

God bent the heavens. The earth moved. The whole world shook. God's glory passed through the four gates: fire, earthquake, storm, and hail.

All the kings of the earth were scared. They sent for Balaam, the soothsayer. They asked him if God was ready to send another flood and wipe out the world. Balaam, told them, "Fools, God promised never to do that again! Instead, God is giving the Chosen People the Torah." All of the kings then shouted together: "Praised be Adonai who blesses God's people with peace." Feeling better, each king went home.

From the Midrash: Mekhilta Rs 85 and 99

As soon as **God** said, "**Anokhi**," the first word in the **Ten Commandments**, there was absolute silence. All of **Creation** was completely quiet. The birds didn't chirp or fly. Oxen didn't bellow. The ocean was still and silent. All creatures were quiet. Even the heavenly angels stopped singing, "**Kadosh Kadosh Kadosh Kadosh Kadosh Kadosh**…. Only **God's Voice** could be heard in the entire world.

From the Midrash: Exodus Rabbah 29.5

The families of Israel saw **God's Voice** as well as heard it. They actually saw the sound waves emerge from **God's Mouth** as waves of fire which traveled around the entire camp of Israel and came to each Jew individually. Each Jew was asked by the Voice, "Do you accept this commandment and all the values it teaches?" And to each commandment, each Jew answered, "Yes."

From the Midrash: Midrash Hazit

B.J.: That's exactly what I remember!

Kent: It sounded like a marriage, where God went to each Jew and said, "Do you take this commandment to be your lawful….:

God said all the **Ten Commandments** together at once, as if they were just one word.

The Midrash: Rokeyah

God said all of the **Ten Commandments** simultaneously in all the **70 languages** spoken in the world.

From the Midrash: Exodus Rabbah 28.5

As loud as **God's Voice** was, it had no echo. Everyone heard the **Commandments** directly from **God's Mouth**.

From the Midrash: Shir ha-Shirim Rabbah 29.9

Chapter 6:
The Ten Commandments

THE FIRST FIVE COMMANDMENTS

Shane L: The first five commandments are about God, the second five are about people.

Davida: The first five are like Jewish ones and holy ones, while the other five are like neighbor things.

1.

I AM **ADONAI**, YOUR GOD,

THE ONE WHO BROUGHT YOU OUT OF THE LAND OF EGYPT

—OUT OF SLAVERY.

2

YOU WILL **NOT** HAVE ANY OTHER GODS BEFORE **ME**.

YOU WILL **NOT** MAKE ANY **IDOLS**.

DO **NOT** BOW DOWN TO **IDOLS** OR SERVE THEM.

3

DO **NOT** USE THE NAME OF *ADONAI*, YOUR GOD,

WHEN MAKING A **FALSE PROMISE**.

4

REMEMBER **SHABBAT**. MAKE IT HOLY.

YOU CAN LABOR FOR SIX DAYS AND DO ALL YOUR WORK.

BUT THE SEVENTH DAY IS **SHABBAT**.

5

HONOR YOUR **FATHER** AND YOUR **MOTHER**.

Which of the Commandments do you think is most important? Why?

____

____

I AM ADONAI YOUR GOD

Shane P: I think "I AM ADONAI YOUR GOD" is the most important commandment, because God is the One who created us, made us, and helped us in our needs.

Kent: "I AM ADONAI YOUR GOD", because without God you wouldn't have any of the rest of the commandments. If there were no God, than nothing would be wrong. Murder would be okay because there would be no persuasion.

Andy: I'm not sure what's being commanded in the first commandment.

Abravanel: Nothing is being commanded. This is not a commandment of either belief or action. It is just an introduction to the other commandments to let the families of Israel know Who is commanding them.

Maimonides: This first commandment commands us to believe in God. The mitzvah is to believe that there is a cause and an organizing force behind all existing things.

YOU WILL NOT HAVE ANY OTHER GODS BEFORE ME

Andy: I think this commandment is the second most important—because it important to say that you won't praise another god or make anything else into a god.

This commandment is a lot like commandment number seven. They both say don't have two of one thing. Don't have two gods and don't have two wives.

Kent: After all, the commandments are like a wedding.

DO NOT USE THE NAME OF ADONAI, YOUR GOD, WHEN MAKING A FALSE PROMISE.

Shane L: My most frequent use of God's name is in vain.

Shane P: God doesn't want to be used as a way of getting you out of trouble. God is supposed to be good—not evil.

REMEMBER SHABBAT. MAKE IT HOLY.

Kent: I think this is the second most important commandment, because you work, build, learn, do everything for six days; the Sabbath is the day where you not only have a break, but where you remember what you've done and what you've got left to do. It's your catch-up time and where you acknowledge what you've learned.

HONOR YOUR FATHER AND YOUR MOTHER

Why is this commandment on the "God side" (commandments 1-5) of the Ten Commandments?

Andy: Because your parents are like gods—sort of. Your parents created you.

Shane L: Parents should be your idols?

Kent: No, not idols—but you want to be like them.

Ben: Parents are on the God side, because they gave you life.

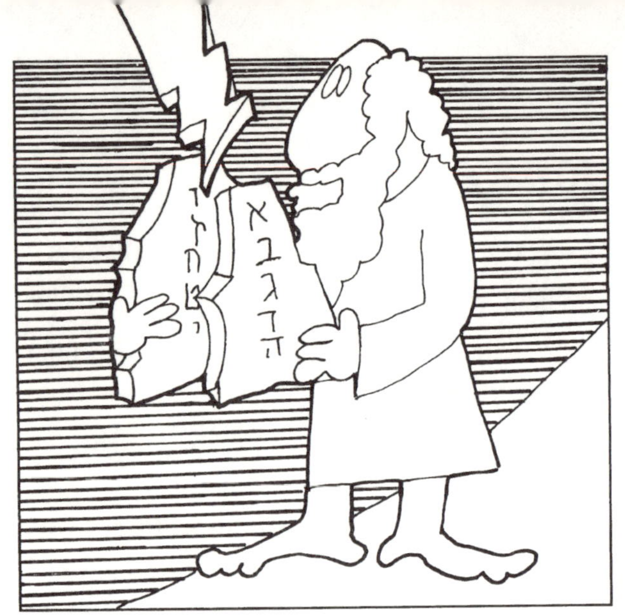

6.

Do NOT **murder**.

7.

Do NOT commit **adultery**.

8.

Do NOT **steal**.

9.

Do NOT **lie** about your neighbor in an oath.

10.

Do NOT **wish** to take over your neighbor's house nor anything which belongs to your neighbor.

DO NOT MURDER.

Shane L: I think this is the second most important commandment, because otherwise you might take someone's life early and they might have something important to live for.

Shane P: What if they die the next day?

Shane L: They can still do something important with that day!

How is this commandment connected to "I AM THE LORD?" That is the first commandment on the "God side"; this is the first commandment on the "People side."

Shane P: Murder is taking away something God created.

Shane L and Kent (at the same time)**:** Killing someone is like killing God, because you were created in God's image.

DO NOT COMMIT ADULTERY.

Shane L: I don't think that this is one of the most important commandments, because people are going to do it. People are going to fall in love with whom they fall in love with, even though it might be fake love or it might be real love!

Shane P: It's usually lust, not love.

DO NOT WISH TO TAKE OVER YOUR NEIGHBOR'S HOUSE NOR ANYTHING WHICH BELONGS TO YOUR NEIGHBOR.

David S.: I think that this is the least important commandment. I think you can feel jealous if you want to, as long as you don't do anything about it.

Kent: I sort of agree and I sort of disagree. I don't think it is wrong to get jealous if you don't do anything about it, but I do think you ought to be thankful for what you have.

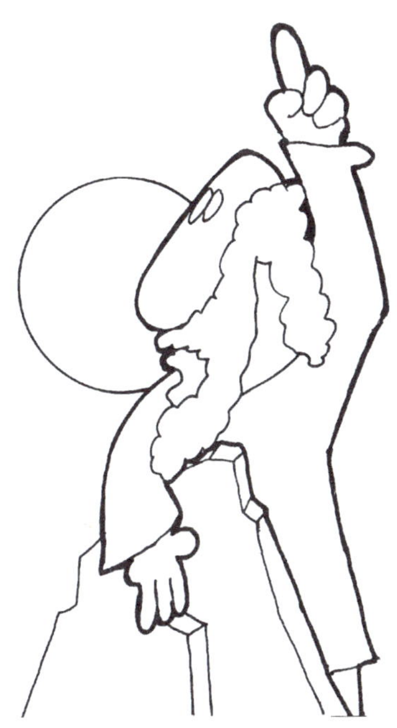

Chapter 7: 40 Days and 40 Nights

From the Torah: Exodus 20:15

From the Torah: Exodus 24:12

AND MOSES WAS ON THE MOUNTAIN FORTY DAYS AND FORTY NIGHTS.

From the Torah: Exodus 24:18

What do you think happened during the 40 days and 40 nights Moses was with God?

____

____

____

Steven Kepler (a guest commentator): When Moses was carving the Ten Commandments, there were these other things he wanted to write down, other ideas about what these commandments mean. At the same time, he was chipping fragments off the big stones. He took the chips, wrote down comments, and tied them on his sandals so they wouldn't get lost.

When Moses came up on high, the angels spoke to The Holy-One-Who-Is-To-Be-Praised, "Ruler-of-the-Cosmos, what is this man born of woman doing among us?"

God answered them, "He has come to receive the Torah."

They said to God, "Are You really going to give him the secret treasure which You have hidden for nine-hundred-and-seventy-four generations—since before the world was created? You are going to give that to flesh and blood?"

Then they sang to God from the Psalms,

WHAT ARE PEOPLE THAT YOU THINK OF THEM?
WHY DO YOU CARE ABOUT THEIR CHILDREN?
O LORD, OUR GOD,

YOUR NAME IS EXCELLENT THROUGH THE EARTH.
YOU HAVE SET YOUR GLORY (THE TORAH) IN THE HEAVENS.

The Holy-One-Who-Is-To-Be-Praised then said to Moses, "Answer them!"

He said, "Ruler-Of-The-Cosmos, I am afraid that they will burn me up with their breaths of fire."

God said to Moses, "Hold on to my Throne-Of-Glory and answer them!"

If you were Moses, and you had to prove to God and the angels that the Jewish people deserved the Torah, how would you do it?

____

____

____

____

Moses did so and said, "Ruler-Of-The-Cosmos, in Your Torah it says, "I am the Lord Your God Who brought you out of the Land of Egypt." (Exodus 20)

Moses then said to the angels, "Did you go down to Egypt? Were you enslaved by Pharaoh? Why should the Torah be yours?"

He went on, "It also says in the Torah 'You shall have no other gods.' Do you live among people who worship idols?"

"It says in the Torah, 'Remember the Shabbat to keep it holy.' Do you do work? Do you need rest?"

"It says in the Torah, 'Do not swear falsely by God's name.' Do you have business? Do you have reasons to cheat and lie?"

"It says in the Torah, 'Honor your father and mother.' Do you have parents? It says, 'You shall not murder. You shall not commit adultery. You shall not steal.' Has any of you ever been jealous? Does any of you ever struggle with a Yetzer ha-Ra (evil impulse)?"

Instantly, the angels loved Moses. They voiced no more protests. Each angel taught Moses a secret. Even the Angel-Of-Death taught Moses his two secrets: tzedakah and t'shuvah (repentance).

Shabbat 88b